What's in a Cave?

by Martha E. H. Rustad

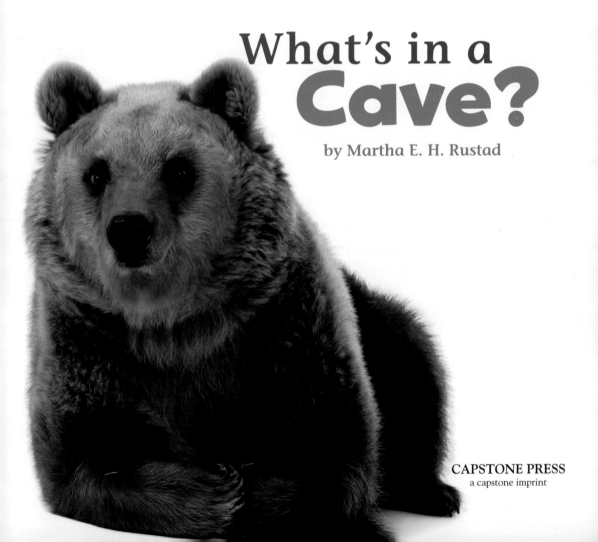

CAPSTONE PRESS
a capstone imprint

Little Pebble is published by Capstone Press,
1710 Roe Crest Drive, North Mankato, Minnesota 56003
www.capstonepub.com

Library of Congress Cataloging-in-Publication Data
Rustad, Martha E. H. (Martha Elizabeth Hillman), 1975– author.
 What's in a cave? / By Martha E. H. Rustad.
  pages cm.—(Little pebble. What's in there?)
 Summary: "Simple nonfiction text and full-color photographs present animals and plants found in a cave"—Provided by the publisher.
 Audience: Ages 5–7 Audience: K to grade 3
 Includes bibliographical references and index.
 ISBN 978-1-4914-6009-2 (library binding)—ISBN 978-1-4914-6021-4 (pbk.)—
 ISBN 978-1-4914-6033-7 (ebook pdf)
 1. Cave animals—Juvenile literature. 2. Caves—Juvenile literature. I. Title. II. Title: What is in a cave?
 QL117.R87 2016
 591.75'84—dc23   2015001934

For Bernice Rose, Oliver Kyle, and Milton Richard.—MEHR

Editorial Credits
Erika L. Shores, editor; Cynthia Della-Rovere, designer; Svetlana Zhurkin, media researcher; Katy LaVigne, production specialist

Photo Credits
Alamy: David Hosking, 9; Dreamstime: Ivkuzmin, 7; iStockphoto: antos777, 17; Minden Pictures: Ingo Arndt, 11, Michael & Patricia Fogden, 19, Phil Chapman, 21; Newscom: Design Pics/Sean White, 5; Shutterstock: Eric Isselee, back cover (top), 1, Jjustas, cover, Koollapan, 15, Nik Merkulov, back cover (bottom) and throughout, Olga Nikonova, 2–3 and throughout, Sue Robinson, 13

Printed in China
042015 008832LEOF15

Table of Contents

Cave Visitors

Shine a light.

Look inside!

What lives in a cave?

Bats hang.

Cave insects eat

bat poop.

A bird makes a nest
from spit and grass.
The nest sticks
to cave walls.

cave swiftlet

Shh!

Bears sleep.

They rest here

all winter.

Cave Plants

Hello, sunshine!

Ferns and mosses need sun.

They grow near

cave openings.

13

Look up!

Tree roots grow down.

They hang in caves.

14

15

A Cave Home

Splash!

A river flows in this cave.

Cave fish swim by.

They have no eyes.

Glow worms shine
in the dark.
Their light brings
prey near.

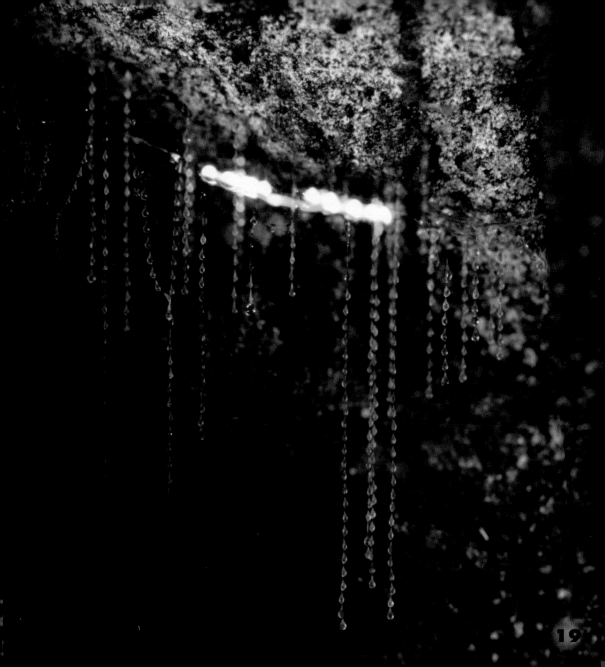

19

Blind spiders feel
with tiny hairs.
Long legs climb over rocks.

Caves make good homes.

Glossary

blind—unable to see

fern—a plant with long leaves that grows in shady, damp places

moss—a small, furry plant that does not have roots or flowers

prey—an animal that is eaten as food

root—a plant part that grows under the soil and sucks up water

Read More

Salzmann, Mary Elizabeth. *Home Sweet Cave.* Sandcastle. Minneapolis: ABDO, 2012.

Spilsbury, Richard. *Look Inside a Cave.* Chicago: Heinemann, 2013.

Wood, Alix. *Gruesome Animals in the Ground.* Earth's Grossest Animals. New York: Windmill Books, 2014.

Internet Sites

FactHound offers a safe, fun way to find Internet sites related to this book. All of the sites on FactHound have been researched by our staff.

Here's all you do:
Visit *www.facthound.com*
Type in this code: 9781491460092

Index